ISBN: 978129002784

Published by:
HardPress Publishing
8345 NW 66TH ST #2561
MIAMI FL 33166-2626

Email: info@hardpress.net
Web: http://www.hardpress.net

EX LIBRIS

HAND SEWING
L E S S O N S

A Graded Course for Schools and for
the Home.

By Sarah Ewell Krolik

WORK WELL DONE MEANS MORE WORK TO DO

EDUCATIONAL PUBLISHING COMPANY

A Skilful Hand is a Helping Hand.

PREFACE.

The value of these lessons has been proven by fifteen years of experience in the "Self-Help Circle," a school organized to instruct girls in the domestic arts. At first they were taught on clothing for themselves, which they paid for in small sums from week to week.

It was found that while all learned to make garments for home use, few became expert needlewomen. Haste to complete wearing apparel resulted in inferior workmanship. A combination course was adopted which gives variety with continuity. It has been used for several years with excellent results. Pupils are taught that only by careful practice can they hope to excel, that these models are the way marks of their progress, and will be treasured by them in the future as their own handiwork. With the text, they form a book of reference on making and mending garments that is highly prized.

"Hand Sewing Lessons" is a book for those who wish to learn sewing and how to teach it to others. It gives a practical course for normal and high school classes and supplies trained teachers with printed instructions for pupils in place of written ones that take so much time and that overlap the work of other departments. The stitches are combined for practice while new ones are being learned, so as to form a continuous line of progress and carry out the principle of bridging the way from the known to the unknown, and of making a pleasant road to knowledge, which will become a part of daily life in after years.

Thanks are due to Mrs. Edwin E. Leggett of Detroit, former superintendent of the Solvay Sewing School, Delray, Michigan, for suggestions from her school notes and plan of finger exercises, and to Mrs. Julia d'Arcambal Giddings for her assistance.

S. E. K.

CONTENTS.

PART FIRST.

DIVISION I.

DIVISION II.

DIVISION III.

PART SECOND.

DIVISION IV.

DIVISION V.

DIVISION VI.

DIVISION VII.

PART THIRD.

DIVISION VIII.

DIVISION IX.

INTRODUCTION.

TO TEACHERS.

Hand Sewing Lessons is a three years' course from which selections can be made for shorter courses. Normal and high school classes complete it in one year of two lessons per week.

With less practice work the entire course can be taken by pupils in two school years.

Models and materials for small articles are supplied by the school. Cloth for garments is supplied by pupils or sold to them at cost. Only plain small garments are made. Pupils are not required to do more practice work than is necessary to acquire skill. If progress is slow, a change from one stitch to another and back again is helpful.

Large classes are taught by passing from one pupil to another in regular order or by receiving at a desk in groups of two or three, those that require assistance. To secure the best results, a class should not number more than fifteen or twenty. Children who are beginners in sewing make, during the first year, simple garments and articles that give practice on the stitches of Part First and make the models included in it, as soon as the sewing is satisfactory. Each child prepares as much of her own work as is possible. This plan is continued through the course.

Pupils sit erect while sewing, with their feet on the floor and the lower part of the spine against the chair back. They should have low chairs and, if possible, tables or desks. Never allow them to pin the work to the knee. Watch the position of the hands, also the manner of holding cloth and implements, until they are held in the right way. Practice is given on pieces of cloth with needles threaded and without knots. A few minutes' exercise in pushing the needle with the thimble is given when the class opens.

Rapidity may be acquired by putting the needle in carefully and drawing it through quickly. Practice this exercise without a knot in the thread.

Teach pupils to sew with the side of the thimble, as it presents a larger surface for wear and can be used with greater ease than the end. The top thimble is objectionable for continuous work, as it retains the perspiration of the finger.

Fine handmade garments are shown them as they progress, to stimulate a desire to improve. Sewing on small articles of use interests a child, and she does not get tired of it, and become careless, nor get in too great haste to finish her work, as is the case in garment making. The latter is taught after some skill and patience are acquired by making simpler things.

Look over the stitches before the school hour and clip threads at short intervals on all that must be ripped.

Great patience should be exercised with dull pupils. Without patience, cheerfulness, and firmness there can be no success. Enthusiasm may be aroused if the teacher understands her work and is in love with it, and loves the children placed in her care.

Mission schools, divided into small classes and taught by volunteer teachers, should be under the supervision of an experienced needlewoman, who is a competent teacher. This method gives the volunteer helper work with which she can make herself familiar and she can get good results by studying to make it interesting. She should come to her class early or provide a substitute who understands sewing. Before the class opens she should see that her pupils have work, so that no time need be lost.

These schools are sometimes organized as clubs. Dues of five cents per quarter, that is, for three months, should be paid by the pupils at the beginning of each term for club funds to be used for material or other small expenses. It gives them a sense of personal ownership in the school to pay something for what they are receiving. No charity should be dispensed, but some special privileges or useful gifts may be given on the last session of each month to those who have attended regularly during that time.

Samples for practice work can be procured for mission schools from wholesale dry goods stores, and some of these pieces are of sufficient value to distribute at the end of each month to pupils whose attendance merits them.

Volunteer teachers should take these lessons from a skilled needle-woman. If they have had experience in sewing they do not need the practice work.

Capable teachers and careful superintendence are essential.

TO MOTHERS.

Sewing should become a part of every girl's education, from childhood to womanhood; not only as a useful art to be practiced at home, but for its educational value. By this means skill and attention are developed, habits of industry are acquired, and a love is cultivated for other domestic arts, which are irksome only to those who have not had any kind of manual training. A prominent educator said that one of the future dangers of our country lies in the habit of idleness resulting from the one-sided education of the present day. As a child can be taught to be generous by teaching it to give, it can be taught to be industrious by teaching it to work, if the teaching is begun early, and if the work is made attractive.

The small boy is quite as much helped by this training as his sister. The needle is used first to string beads. Children draw simple things on white cardboard, four or five inches square, and make pin holes on the lines about one-quarter inch apart. They can easily sew through these with a needle which should be threaded with bright cotton for first work, and later with silk or wool.

A girl of three or four years of age is pleased to sew daily. Give her a needle with a double thread, or a coarse needle, so that it can pass through the cloth easily when the thread is tied to it. The cloth should be thin, with some dressing in it, or coarse and loosely woven. At first she will take a few stitches over and over, the thread will tangle, and she will soon tire. Do not be discouraged by her failures. Daily efforts will soon make her more skilful and she will be able to sew a seam if a line is marked along the edge for the stitches. They will be of uneven length, but do not rip them. Draw another line near the first and let her try again. Allow her to

13

sew often, but not more than fifteen minutes at a time. It may be a year before she can sew a seam well, but all the while she is learning to concentrate her mind. Develop self-reliance by encouraging her to make her own choice of colors and to decorate her doll's gowns with bits of ribbon, according to her own fancy.

By the time she is four years old she will be able to join strips of cloth and wind them into balls to be made into a rag carpet rug for the nursery. Cut the rags of bright pieces of cotton or silk which can be saved in a box for that purpose. Give her a covered basket for her work and teach her to keep it in order. She should have a pair of blunt scissors and be allowed to cut paper over a box or open newspaper, and should put away the scraps. She will make what she imagines to be familiar figures of all sorts and will soon learn to cut by a line on paper or on pieces of striped gingham or calico, and to cut strips for weaving dolls' rugs.

She will enjoy cutting flowers from wall paper for decorations, and pictures of children from advertisements, for paper dolls, and it will be fine practice.

Keep the work basket handy for a spare moment and her box of supplies well filled. Make the sewing a part of every day's routine to be taken in hand several times, if possible. As she grows older a regular time may be set.

When she is eight years old, or perhaps before, she can cut doll's clothes of paper and fit them on a paper doll with library paste. She can also design and make them of cloth for her dolls.

By this time she may be able to make the first models, and she will have skill and application that will be of use to her. If her needle is a rival of her books, so much the better. Books will have their time a little later and she will be better prepared to devote herself to them then, for idleness will be irksome. She will bring to them that concentration of mind so lacking in many girls of to-day, whose hands were not educated with their brains.

For variety and to develop thought and skill, interest the child in the useful occupations of making household articles and furniture by encouraging her to manufacture them in miniature form. The dry goods box or

14

doll-house, with its three floors and garret under a Gothic roof, may be furnished with the work of little hands, and with care and perseverance it will put on an attractive appearance. Rugs may be woven for it, and by the exercise of ingenuity in the use of cloth, clay, wood, and paper, articles for ornament and use in corresponding size may be provided.

Young girls who are being taught to sew in school should receive the careful attention of the mother, as the time allowed in most schools is too short for the necessary training. The teacher is greatly helped by her co-operation. Girls enjoy taking this course at home. An older member of the family, with some knowledge of hand sewing, can easily qualify herself to give it. Mothers are amply repaid for their efforts, by the benefits which their daughters derive from domestic training in all the arts of home making, and sewing is a very important one.

HAND SEWING LESSONS.

A Graded Course for Schools.

TOPICS FOR TALKS.

Object lessons are given on the following articles used in sewing — silk, wool, linen, cotton, and their manufacture into cloth, batting, cord, thread, and yarn; also needles, pins, thimbles, emery, scissors, buttons, wax, hooks and eyes. The difference between gingham and calico, between plain and twilled cloth, and between wool and silk, is explained.

Cabinets are prepared showing the changes from the raw material to the finished article.

SEWING OUTFIT.

Pupils should have aprons, books for models, paper and cloth to practice on, thimbles, scissors, and measures of their own, and thread, needles, pins, wax, and emery balls for desks or for class use at tables. Convenient boxes are of strong, thin Manila cardboard, that close like envelopes, and fasten with a string. They are seven inches wide, ten inches long, and one inch high. If strong Manila envelopes are used, they should be about two inches wider. Cloth bags are also used. They are drawn up with an open string, the ends of which are wound around the top in opposite directions and tied. A case of pigeon-holes is convenient for storing work-boxes. Use a rubber band to hold the leaves containing the models. Cut sixty-inch cloth measures into ten-inch lengths to supply classes.

Cloth is a woven or felted fabric.

A selvedge is the woven edge of cloth.

A raw edge is one that is cut or torn.

A seam is a line formed to join two pieces of fabric.

A nap is a surface of fine hair or fiber combed from the cloth, and lying smoothly in one direction.

The lengthwise threads are called the warp. It is parallel with the selvedge.

The crosswise threads are called the woof. It runs from selvedge to selvedge.

A bias is a slanting line across warp and woof.

A true bias is one that has the same angle to the warp that it has to the woof.

The warp is nearly always stronger and firmer than the woof, and shrinks more when washed.

The woof usually stretches more than the warp. As woof will stretch, make this test when pieces are to be joined with warps parallel. Cut off selvedge edges when not required, or clip them at intervals.

Cloth sometimes becomes crooked when pressed at a factory. It is straight when you can ravel the torn edges. If it does not seem straight, stretch it diagonally until it is. Cloth tears more easily lengthwise than crosswise. Cloth for hand sewing should be soft, and not too closely woven for the needle to pass through it easily. Cut linen on the line of a drawn thread and ginghams by a thread of the pattern.

NEEDLES AND THREAD.

Thread is a small twist of linen, silk, cotton, or wool.

A needle is a small wire of steel, with a sharp point at one end, and a hole at the other.

18

Needles are sharps, betweens, and blunts. Sharps are used for millinery, for light weight cloth, and for basting. Blunts and betweens are used for heavy weight cloth.

Use the best quality. Never use a bent needle.

Use Nos. 30 and 40 thread with No. 7 needles.

Use Nos. 40 and 50 thread with No. 8 needles.

Use Nos. 60 and 70 thread with No. 9 needles.

Use Nos. 80 and 90 thread with No. 10 needles.

Use Nos. 90 and 100 thread with No. 11 needles.

Use No. 100 and finer threads with No. 12 needles.

Use thread to match in size the thread of the material.

Use thread no longer than the arm. Thread for button-holes may be two-thirds of that length. Never bite or break the thread from a garment.

A small knot in the thread is allowable when it can be hidden. To prevent kinking, make the knot on the end that breaks from the spool. Silk thread should be fastened securely.

A class needle-book can be made by folding up one inch of a five-inch square of felt, and stitching places for different sizes of needles. Mark the number above each place, and finish the edge with blanket-stitch.

MODELS.

Paper patterns of the models are cut by the pupils, and the edges are turned and folded as directed. Bias folds are cut from newspapers or striped paper. Calico, gingham, and colored paper are used for the first practice in cutting. The narrow blade of the shears is held below the material to be cut. A pupil is taught to hold the point toward herself when passing a needle, knife, or shears to others. The models are drawn on the board, and explained by the teacher before they are made, and by the pupil afterward. The calico, gingham, and cotton used are of medium quality. Make patterns of firm gingham, or use the first model cut, to secure exactness. It should be marked for that purpose.

The models are carefully cut by the teacher, or by advanced pupils under her supervision. Strips for the models are torn lengthwise. Remove the selvedge, measure carefully, allow for threads that will ravel, cut ½ inch slash by the thread, and tear off a strip. When the models are used for practice, they are cut at a garment factory. In this course, the stitches are practiced on simple articles for use until the desired standard is reached. When the models are made, paste or pin them in a book, and write above each its number and the page that explains it. Use the right hand pages of the Manila leaves for the models, and the left for best practice work. Place samples of the material used on the first page.

COMBINATION OF GRADED COURSE WITH PRACTICE WORK.

The fabric used for practice in learning stitches is graded from coarse to fine. They are taught in groups of two or three on articles that are suitable for the skill acquired.

The following outline includes such as are easily prepared and will suggest others.

PART FIRST.

Practice cutting squares and strips of colored paper, rags for weaving and patterns of the models in Part First.

MODEL 1 is on a bright strip of calico, with dots ¼ inch apart, through which the needle passes. It pleases the child, and is something that she can do, and is to do exactly as directed. By the time these stitches are taken, she will know what ¼ of an inch is, and this knowledge will help her measure with her eyes and to baste with $\frac{1}{4}$ inch stitches. The manufacture of cotton cloth is explained and a hand loom is shown, on which is a warp partly woven with wool, raffia, or fine rags to illustrate warp, woof, and selvedge, as they are to become familiar terms.

PRACTICE FOR MODELS 2, 3, and 4. OVERHANDING AND OVERCASTING. Overhanding is the best practice to develop skill with the needle.

Make French hems on towels and light-colored calico dust-cloths. The French hem is basted, turned back to the line for the hem, and overhanded. Overhand the patches for a doll's quilt for first attempts and vary the size by joining four or five, or many more, according to the skill acquired. Turn the edges back evenly $\frac{3}{8}$ of an inch, baste in $\frac{1}{4}$ inch stitches, and overhand. After this practice in handling the needle, a sofa-pillow cover in turkey red and bright blue calico may be overhanded in strips or squares. The cloth is cut at a garment factory in $2\frac{1}{2}$ by 5 inch lengthwise strips. Alternate the colors and overhand the ends together with four strips in the first row, and a half strip at each end of the second row, to form a brick pattern. In joining the half pieces, care is taken to have the warps parallel. Four strips, $\frac{1}{8}$ yard in width, torn across the cloth, will make ruffles for the four sides of each pillow cover, if the corners are left open. Double the ruffles or hem them, gather each with a double thread in two rows of fine running stitches, baste to the cover and sew in half-backstitch. Sew the back on afterward to make the work easier for hand sewing.

PILLOW COVER DESIGN FOR CHILDREN'S WORK. Alternate and overhand three blue and four red $2\frac{1}{2}$ inch squares to form a strip. Four of these strips and three of same size in blue are joined by backstitch, after the ruffles are made. Give lessons in hemming and in running stitch on simple articles. Make the ruffles as above and join the parts of the cover. (See pages, 72, 99.)

Other articles may be substituted to provide the necessary practice in overhanding, if more desirable, and the work may be varied by making sachet, thimble and button bags of silk with silk thread. Make pincushions of flowered sateens or other fancy goods cut square or heart-shaped. Baste the edges separately, lay batting between the sides to fill lightly, baste for overhanding and handle carefully. Make book covers of coarse linen or cretonne. Practice overcasting on ruled paper, cut off, and repeat until some progress is made.

Make Models 1 to 4, and overcast them.

PRACTICE FOR MODELS 5 AND 6. RUNNING AND TUCKING. Practice position of hands, by sewing on a fold of cloth.

Make double or threefold washcloths of cheesecloth. Baste, and join with running stitch, turn, run the opening together, and ornament the edges with two or three rows of running stitch in blue thread. Make initials in running stitch and sew on a hanger.

Baste and run hems in cheesecloth dust-cloths. When finished, baste the maker's name on each, and place in the care of the teacher, to be feather-stitched later as practice for Model 23. Make bags of soft material, to hold soiled handkerchiefs, dust-cloths, or the weekly darning. Sew the sides, and spaces for the draw-strings, in running stitch, and overcast the raw edges. Leave an opening on each side for the tapes. Overhand the hems before running the spaces. Run hems on cheap, sheer lawn for handkerchiefs. Make a doll's apron of the same, 6x7 inches in size. Run ⅛ inch hems at the sides, a ½ inch hem at the top to be drawn up with ribbon and an inch hem at the bottom. Ornament the latter with a simple design in running stitch. This is made by children in place of the running model, 5 (*a*) and (*b*). (See page 72.)

Make Models 5 and 6.

PRACTICE FOR MODELS 7 AND 8. HEMMING. Hem towels and kitchen aprons. Hem blue or red ruffles for the sofa pillows, sheets and pillow cases for a child's bed, and handkerchiefs. A square of 40 inch India linon will make nine handkerchiefs. This is also a practical width for aprons. Hem plain aprons of all kinds, from coarse to fine. Hem the tops to carry ties of ribbon or tape.

A doll's apron of the given size is hemmed at the top to carry a ribbon. The bottom is hemmed on the right side and turned up 1½ inches to form a row of four pockets.

Make Models 7 and 8.

PRACTICE FOR MODEL 9. HEM-STITCHING. Hem-stitch hand towels, bands of scrim for collars and cuffs, sheets and pillow cases of coarse, loosely-woven cotton or butcher's linen for doll's bed, centerpiece and napkins of same material for doll's table, and hem-stitch tray cloths. Ruffles for doll's underskirts may be hemmed or hem-stitched.

Make Model 9.

PART SECOND.

PRACTICE FOR MODELS 10 TO 14. BACKSTITCHING, HALF-BACKSTITCHING, COMBINATION STITCHES, GATHERING AND GAUGING. Backstitch duck or denim holders, beanbags, or other articles of coarse material. Stitch the outlines of a design on a 5 inch square of firm, unbleached cotton. Bind circular button bags to be drawn up from opposite sides. They can be opened wide when needed.

A doll is now introduced. Garments are fitted to it, which are given to the makers when finished. Join the parts of doll's gored skirt with French seams, make and lay the gathers, and join the ruffle with a faced hem. Use placket Model 13 (a). Make and lay gathers of skirt, and put on the band. Make children's drawers with flat fell (see Illustration 14), and 13 (b) plackets. Put on bands and baste the hems. They can be hemmed for busy work, while pupils are waiting for the attention of the teacher, and will supply practice later for button-holes. Dolls', or infants', plain nightgowns may take the place of the children's drawers, or be made for additional practice. To make infant's piqué shoes and slippers, backstitch a double bias fold of lawn along the edges and hem the folded edge of the bias strip on the wrong side to form a narrow binding around the parts. Overhand them together. Doll's waists with drawers to button on, are Models 29 and 30. Make them after the above practice and finish with buttons and button-holes, after practice for Model 15.

Make Models 10 to 14.

PRACTICE FOR MODEL 15. BUTTON–HOLES. Button-holes are made on a strip of firm bleached cotton, 2x6 inches. Fold lengthwise, trim and overcast the raw edges, and buttonhole the folded edge. Cut ½ inch button-holes, one inch apart, in the strip, and work them. This practice may be used for a contest. Make button-holes on the drawers and on the doll's garments. Give as much practice as is necessary.

Make Model 15.

MODELS 16, 17, AND 18. MATCHING AND MENDING. These models are practiced on the gingham squares until satisfactory.

MODELS 19 AND 20. Gussets and nightshirt fronts are omitted by children and taught later with garment making.

PART THIRD.

PRACTICE FOR MODEL 21. WEAVING AND DARNING. Weave on looms. They may be made of cardboard, 4x5 inches in size, with holes punched at each end to hold the warp in place. Practice darning on light colored stockinet, and tie square knots on the holders with several coarse threads in a large needle. Teach the square knot with a large, soft cord.

Make Model 21.

MODEL 22. FRENCH HEM AND DARNING ON TABLE LINEN. Practice the French hems on napkins and towels. Darning on linen is omitted by children.

Make Model 22.

PRACTICE FOR MODEL 23. FEATHER-STITCH AND OTHER FANCY STITCHES. Feather-stitch a lengthwise strip of dotted cloth and the dust-cloths. If the calico dust-cloths are dotted the dots may be followed on the lengthwise sides. Feather-stitch dust-cloths, the ruffles of the sofa pillow covers, the doll's sheets and pillow cases, and the other articles that have been made.

Children, omit (b) and (c) of Model 23, fagoting.

Make Model 23.

PRACTICE FOR MODELS 24 AND 25. SLIP-STITCH, PURL EDGE, DARNING ON CASHMERE, BLANKET, FLANNEL, AND CAT STITCHES. Make holes in piece of cashmere and darn them, stamp and embroider bottoms of doll's flannel skirts. Sew the seams with two running stitches and a backstitch, press them open and fasten with a row of flannel-stitch on each side. To make the plackets, fold back ½ inch on the left sides, and ¼ inch on the right sides, and cat-stitch the raw edges to hold them. See Model 13 (a). Pleat and finish with bands, buttons and button-holes. Make a heart-shaped sachet or pincushion. Baste the edges of the top and bottom separately, place the cotton and sachet between, baste the edges together, and finish with blanket-stitch. Make the blanket-stitch on the leaves and covers of a needle-book.

Make Models 24 and 25.

Practice for Model 26. Cross-stitching. Cross-stitch initials on doll's garments and sheets.

Make Model 26.

Practice for Model 27. Rolled Ruffle and Gathers. Overhand lace on handkerchiefs. Make ruffle for doll's dress.

Model 27 is omitted by children.

Model 28. Doll's Gored Skirt.

Model 29. Doll's Underwaist.

Model 30. Doll's Drawers.

Model 31. Doll's Flannel Skirt.

Model 32. Doll's Dress.

If Model 27 has been omitted, the ruffle for the dress may be hemmed, hem-stitched, or feather-stitched.

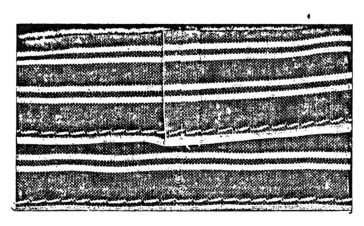

Illustration 2. Both sides of a matched seam.
A Section of Model 3.

This seam shows in a line down the center. The top of the pieces joined is folded over to show the wrong side. The right side of the seam extends below and may be seen if looked for closely. A patch carefully inserted in this way escapes the eye.

26

PART FIRST.

Division I. Basting, Overhanding, and Overcasting.

MODEL I. BASTING.

A lengthwise strip of bright red calico, 5x7 inches, with white or black dots, ¼ inch apart. Fold through the middle, parallel with the warp on a row of dots, and hold the two sides together evenly with a row of ½ inch basting stitches taken close to the raw edge of the long side, to be removed when the model is ready for overcasting. If the pupil has had no practice in sewing, this piece is

prepared as above and placed in her hands, with the folded edge held up, the knot on the under side, and the needle in the second row of dots.

Baste closely for hand work, with stitches of such length as the

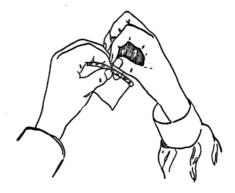

Illustration 3. A Section of Model I. Illustration 4. Hands in position for overhanding.

27

material requires. All basting should be done evenly. Cut basting threads freely before removing them.

MODEL 2. OVERHANDING.

Two pieces of calico, 2x4 inches, in contrasting colors. Two pieces of cotton, 2x4 inches.

(*a*) Fold back one side of each piece of calico $\frac{3}{16}$ of an inch, lay the right sides together, and baste with $\frac{1}{4}$ inch stitches. Hold the work in the left hand, between the forefinger slightly curved and the thumb held straight. Hide the knot under the fold, point the needle directly toward you, and sew from right to left. Practice until the stitches are made fine, even, and close to the edge. To avoid knots, after the practice has been given, overcast the ends of the thread with the seam.

(*b*) Repeat on cotton and overcast.

Use No. 60 red thread and No. 9 needle for overhanding and overcasting the cotton model.

Fasten the thread by passing it under the point of the needle when the last stitch is taken, or sew two or three stitches in the same place.

MODEL 3. MATCHED EDGES OVERHANDED.

Two pieces of striped gingham or calico, 2x4 inches. The stripes should cross the pieces, be equi-distant from each end, and be joined to match. Follow directions of Model 2 for overhanding.

MODEL 4. WARP AND WOOF. OVERCASTING.

Four pieces of calico, 2½ inches square, two of them of a light, and two of contrasting color.

Plain, bright-colored cottons may be used. Striped cotton is not used in this model, as lines would denote the warp, which the pupil is required to determine for herself.

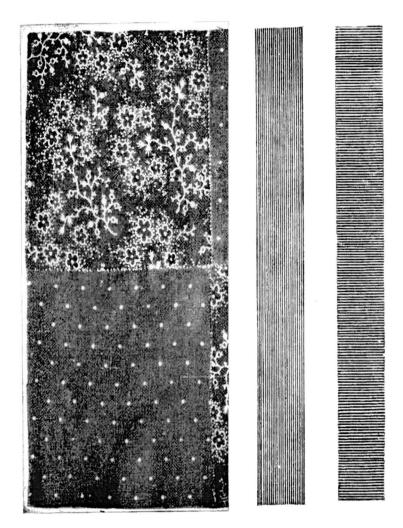

Illustration 5. A Section of Model 4.   Illustration 6. Warp (*a*). Woof (*b*).

Form a square by alternating the two colors, with warp parallel
to warp. Follow previous directions for overhanding. Practice
overcasting on ruled paper. Cut off and repeat until satisfactory,
after which overcast the Models of Division I in colored thread.

Overcast ⅛ inch stitches, ⅛ inch from the raw edges. When
a new thread is required, fasten the end that remains, at the back,

where the next stitch is to be taken, bring it through, and continue as before.

Division II. Running and Tucking.

MODEL 5. RUNNING STITCH.

Cotton, 2½ x 6 inches.

Calico, gingham, or white corded dimity, 5 inches square, with hair stripe ⅛ inch apart.

(*a*) A design is drawn on the cotton by the pupil, to be outlined in running stitch. Turn the edges back, and finish with flannel-stitch. (See Model 25, and Illustration 34, No. 8.)

(*b*) Overcast the square in ⅛ inch stitches, ⅛ inch from the edge. Start at one corner, ¼ inch from the edge, and run six squares, one within the other, ⅛ inch apart, making fine stitches midway between the stripes, and ⅛ inch stitches, when sewing across them, under one stripe and over the next. Straighten each side as directed below.

· Children substitute a doll's apron for this model. See combination of course with practice work.

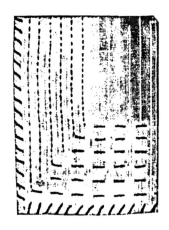
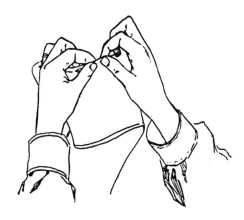

Illustration 7. A Corner of Model 5. Illustration 8. Hands in position for running.

RUNNING SEAM. Take up two or three running stitches, then hold the edge of the cloth and the needle with the right thumb and forefinger, and push the needle with the thimble, while the left thumb and forefinger holds the cloth before the point.

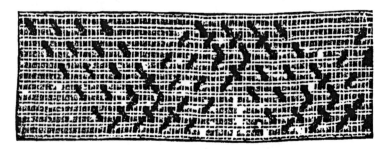

Illustration 9.   Design in running stitch.

A pupil should practice on strips of cloth, and sew, without a knot in her thread, until she can hold the work in her hands properly, and push the needle with her thimble.   Before she makes the model, she should learn to make fine, even stitches, with her hands held in the right position.   Begin running stitch by sewing one stitch over another, and finish in the same way.

To avoid puckering the work, begin at the right hand side before fastening the thread, and smooth the thread from right to left between the left thumb and forefinger before fastening it.

MODEL 6.   TUCKING.

Checked gingham, 5 inches square, cut by the check.

Calico, 5x8 inches, with figures having direction.

(*a*) Tuck the gingham by the check, tucking the alternate dark rows of checks.

(*b*) Ravel a thread from each edge of the calico, to be sure that it is straight.   If it does not seem to be straight, stretch it diagonally until it is.   See that the figures are upright, and crease the edge of the first tuck, 1½ inches from the bottom of the strip.

31

Make ½ inch tucks, with ½ inch spaces between the stitchings. This will bring the bottom of each tuck on a line with the stitching of the tuck below it.

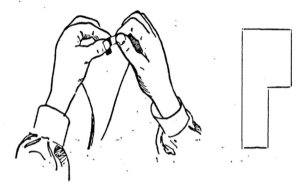

Illustration 10. (*a*) Hands in position for tucking in fine running stitches
(*b*) Measure for Tucks.

Cut a measure, which includes the width of the tuck and the space between the stitchings. Cut the width of the tuck on it. To make a fold for the bottom of the next tuck, measure in two places and crease between.

Give the designs on cloth the same direction when joining the parts of a garment, and see that they are right side up.

Division III. Hemming and Hem-stitching.

MODEL 7. HEMMING. MITRED CORNER.

Striped gingham, or calico, 2x4 inches.

Cotton, 6x8 inches.

(*a*) The stripes should cross the model, and be hemmed exactly on the stripes to which they belong.

Turn ¼ inch hem. Use No. 70 thread and No. 9 needle.

(*b*) Fold inch hems on all sides of the cotton piece — on the long sides first. Mitre the corners at one end of the model. Use a measuring card, crease the folds, and cut the superfluous cloth from

32

the corners. Baste these hems with ¼ inch stitches. The sewing should show as little as possible on the right side.

To start a new thread, take a stitch back of the last one and hide the ends under the fold. Finish the hem by taking two or three stitches over each other, or by sewing through a loop of the thread.

Illustration 11 (*a*). Hands in position for hemming.

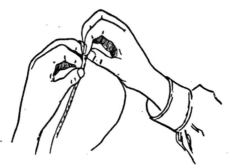

Illustration 11 (*b*). The hem carried between the second and third fingers.

The hem should be held between the left thumb and forefinger until several inches have been hemmed, then passed over the first and second fingers and under the third, but never over one finger. The second and third fingers are used to pull the work over the forefinger as the stitches are taken. The hemming must never be curved over the forefinger at the place where the needle is inserted. Slant the needle as nearly on a line with the hem as possible.

A mitred corner is formed by making a diagonal seam from the outside to the inside corner of the hem. (See illustration 12, *a* and *b*.) Make a paper model. Fold the hem, open the folds, and fold the corner at right angles on the line *a–b*. Cut the corner off on the dotted line ¼ inch from *a–b*. Replace the folds as in Illustration 12 (*b*). Fold and cut the cloth in the same manner, and overhand the diagonal seam. (Illustration 12, *b*.)

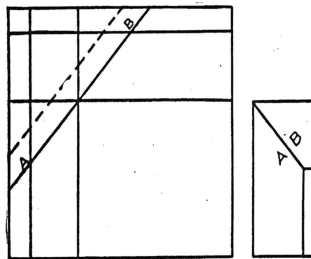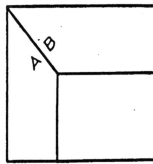

Illustration 12. (*a*) Mitred corner open.   (*b*) Mitred corner, cut and folded.

Wide hems and hems on woolen cloth should have both folds basted.

MODEL 8. EXTENSION AND FACED HEMS.

Cotton, 5 inches square.

Two pieces of cotton, cut crosswise, from a 5 inch square.

Join the strips in running stitch to each end of the first piece, with warp parallel to warp.

(*a*) FACED HEM. Turn one of the joined pieces up the full width and make a blind hem. Baste, take up two threads of the cloth, and pass the needle ⅛ inch inside the fold. Draw through and start the next stitch at the end of the last.

34

(*b*) Extension Hem. Turn the second piece up half way and hem to the seam.

A bias facing should be used on a curved edge. When sewing on a facing by hand, hold it toward you. A binding is a narrow extension hem.

Model 9. Pillow Case. Hem-stitching.

Cotton, 6x7 inches, with selvedge on one of the long sides.

Measure 2⅛ inches along the selvedge for width of hem, and draw five threads of the woof. Turn the raw edges at the top and side, baste and overhand the pillow case on the outside before the hem is turned. The selvedge is used on the side of the pillow case.

Baste the hem on a line with the drawn threads, hold the work lengthwise over the left forefinger and between the left thumb and second finger, and work from left to right.

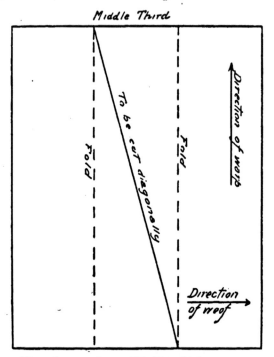

Illustration 13. Square folded into thirds for cutting.

35

Use No. 70 thread and No. 9 needle. Hide the knot under the fold, take up four threads with the needle, draw it through, put the needle in again at the first of the four threads, and take a stitch through the cloth and the folded edge. Draw the thread through forward and downward. When extra strength is required, take a stitch between each cluster.

To make a knotted hem-stitch, use colored thread, and pass it under the needle as it comes through the folded edge, and take a stitch between each cluster. It is made on the right side.

PART SECOND.

Division IV. Backstitching and Combination Stitches.

MODEL 10. BACKSTITCHING, HALF-BACKSTITCHING, AND FELLING.

Cotton, 5 inches square. Cotton, 2½ x 5 inches, cut lengthwise.

Firm, unbleached cotton, 5 inches square, for design in back-stitch (See pages 100, 101.)

Fold the edge back and finish with flannel stitch. (Page 63.)

A backstitch is taken back to form a continuous line of stitches. A half-backstitch is taken half way back. Illustration 14.

Fold the first square lengthwise, and cut as directed in Illustration 13.

Draw a thread of the warp ¼ inch from the edge on the straight side of one of these sections. Backstitch on this line to join the oblong piece, and overcast the seam. Join the bias edges with half backstitch. Have upper edge wider, and baste evenly close to the narrow edge. Sew the seam with the wider edge toward you. Turn the extra width over the narrow edge and hem, so as to cover both edges and form a flat fell. Pink the edges by clipping them when held up and over the end of the forefinger between the thumb and second finger. With practice, this can be done rapidly.

Counter-felling is used in machine sewing, to join parts of garments where a strong seam is required. For example: the side seams of under-waists. Make a ¼ inch fold on the wrong side of one edge to be joined, and one on the right side of the other edge. Place them together, so that the raw edges will be inside, and the

37

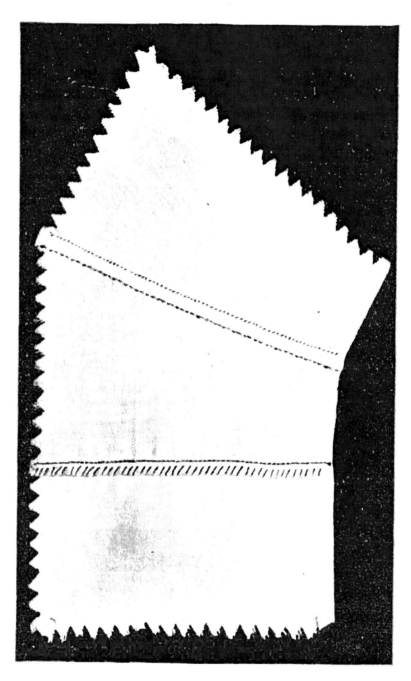

Illustration 14. Represents Model 10.

38

width of the seam will be ½ inch. The folded edges are stitched, if the garment is made by machine, and hemmed, if made by hand.

Double-felling is used when a flat seam is required. Make a narrow hem on each side of the edges to be joined, and overhand the edges of hems, or stitch a seam and hem the edges back on each side of it.

Models 10 and 11 represent:

1. Two straight edges joined with a backstitch.

2. Two bias edges joined with a half-backstitch.

3. A bias and a straight edge joined with two running and a half-backstitch.

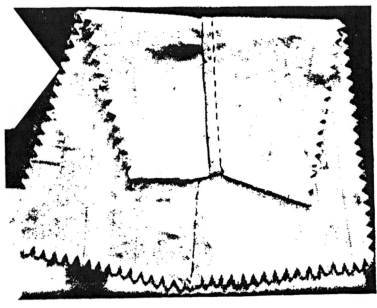

Illustration 15. Represents Model 11.

MODEL 11. A FRENCH SEAM.

Cotton, 5 inches square.

Fold and cut the square as directed in Model 10. Join a bias to a straight edge, lay the narrow ends together, hold the bias edge

39

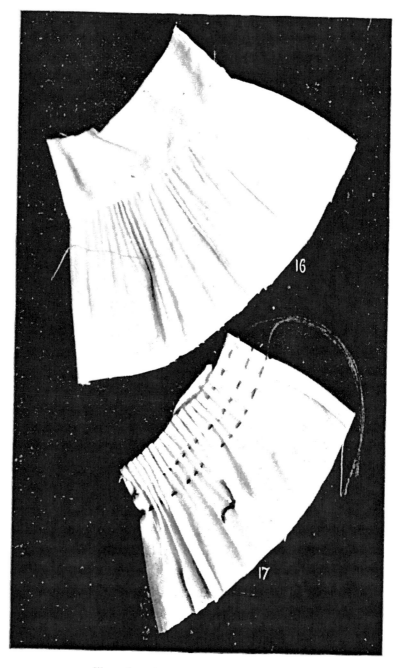

Illustration 16. Hemming gathers on a band.
Illustration 17. The wrong side of gauging partly attached to a band.

40

toward you, join with two running stitches and a half-backstitch in white thread, trim the edges, turn, and sew with the same stitch in red thread.

Use No. 60 thread and No. 8 needle.

MODEL 12. GATHERING AND GAUGING.

Cotton, 5 inches square.

Two lengthwise pieces of cotton: $2\frac{1}{2} \times 1\frac{1}{2}$ inches, band for gathering; $1\frac{1}{2}$ inches square, band for gauging.

Use No. 50 thread and No. 8 needle for gathering and gauging.

Use No. 70 thread and No. 9 needle for hemming.

Hem the sides that are parallel with the warp, double the thread for both gathering and gauging, cut it a little longer than the bands, and take the stitches evenly.

(*a*) Gather $\frac{1}{4}$ inch from the edge, parallel with the woof, and do not draw the needle through until all of the stitches are taken. To lay the gathers, draw them so that they will lie closely together without crowding, insert a pin, and wind the thread about it. Use a No. 6 needle, begin at the left side, and stroke the gathers straight downward, with care not to injure the fabric, and lay them closely between the left thumb and fore-finger. Draw the gathers the size of the band and hold as directed above. Hem each gather to the right side of the band, or hold the gathers toward you and backstitch them. When the gathers are sewed in place, take the pin out and fasten the gathering thread.

(*b*) Gauge this model opposite the gathers. Fold back $\frac{1}{2}$ inch, and crease. Make the stitches $\frac{1}{8}$ inch long, with $\frac{1}{8}$ inch spaces, make the first row $\frac{1}{8}$ inch from the fold, and the rows $\frac{1}{4}$ inch apart. Turn the edges of the band, fold, baste, and overhand the ends. Overhand each stitch of the gauging to the band.

41

Illustration 18. (a) Represents Model 12. Children's model.
(b) Shield for fore-finger of left hand. Used by needle-women.

To lay gathers in thin cloth that has dressing in it, fill the needle with stitches, and press them tightly together before drawing them through. On soft, thin cloth, make two rows of gathers.

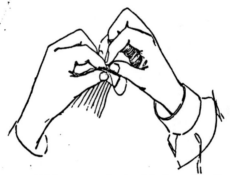

Illustration 19. Joining a gauged strip of cloth to a band in overhand stitch.

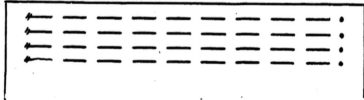

Illustration 20. Stitches ⅛ inch, and spaces ¼ inch, for full gauging.

Gauging is used to draw a large quantity into a small space. The stitches are longer than for gathering, and two or three rows are made, which are directly under each other.

Bands are cut lengthwise. When extra strength is required, cut them longer and fold the ends back to stay the button-holes.

Children omit the gauging on Model 12, make an inch hem in its place and add ties of narrow tape to represent an apron.

MODEL 13. PLACKETS FOR SKIRTS AND DRAWERS.

Cotton, 5 inches square.

Cotton, 4½ x 1 inch, for band of second placket.

Third the square and cut a 2 inch slash down each fold. (See Illustration 13.)

43

(*a*) Make ½ inch hem on one side of the first opening, a narrow hem on the other side, and fasten the wider hem over the other, with two rows of stitching across the angle of the opening.

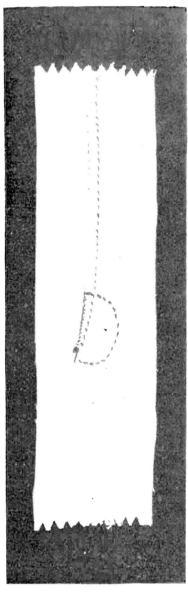

Illustration 21.   Model 14 (*b*).

(*b*) Bind the second opening with the band, fold back the side to be lapped, and extend the other side under it.

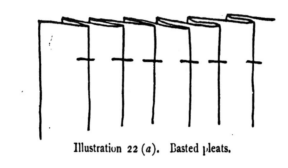

Illustration 22 (*a*). Basted pleats.

Illustration 22 (*b*). Bias strips. Join by overhanding the selvedge edges or by a narrow seam.

MODEL 14. PLACKETS FOR DRESSES.

Cotton, 5 inches square.

Cotton, 2¼ x 1 inch, for facing the first placket.

Cotton, 2¼ x 1½ inches, for extension hem of second placket.

(*a*) Make a faced hem on the upper side, and an extension hem on the under side. Fasten the angle as directed above.

(*b*) Make a narrow hem on both edges of the second opening, and fold back ½ inch on the side to be lapped over. Lay the right side of the hems together, and stitch a half circle on the wrong side to fasten the angle of the opening.

Division V.

MODEL 15. BUTTON-HOLES, EYELETS, THREAD-EYES, AND SEWING ON TAPES, BUTTONS, HOOKS AND EYES.

A lengthwise piece of firm cotton, 2x6 inches, for practice.

Two lengthwise pieces of the same, 2x4 inches.

A button-hole is cut on the line of a thread, and curved around the front end to hold the shank of the button. The back is straight, and is held together by a bar of several threads that is covered by sewing over and over them, or by working them with button-hole stitch. A button-hole is cut the width of the button to be used.

Button-holes are cut with button-hole scissors or with a chisel. A ticket punch is sometimes used to cut the round hole at the front. In light or medium weight cloth, this may be done with a bodkin before the button-hole is cut, and the threads clipped that are displaced around the hole.

Overcast with very fine thread, so that the surface of the button-hole will be smooth. When a coarse thread or twist is used to strengthen a button-hole, it is put through from the wrong side, at the end farthest from the edge of the garment and carried around the second and third fingers of the left hand to hold it tight while the button-hole is worked over it. A heavy thread to work the button-hole over may be carried from the back to the front, fastened there with one stitch and carried back to the starting point. Using thread to stay a button-hole is called cording. Take another thread, when that in the needle is not long enough to make a complete button-hole. The stitches should be taken along the line of a thread in the cloth, to keep them even.

Double the strip of cotton lengthwise, baste, and practice button-holing on the folded edge. Cut button-holes 1 inch apart in the strips for practice, and begin at the back — that is, at the end farthest from the fold — hold up the edge to be worked between the left thumb and forefinger, draw the thread through to the edge, take a stitch and pass the thread from left to right under the point of the needle, as in Illustration 34, No. 4, and draw the needle through toward you at right angles to the button-hole, then draw the thread up evenly, so that the purl will be on the edge.

Make the stitches close on the sides, curved around the front, and make a bar across the back.

Overcast the first button-holes. Overcast and cord them when some skill is acquired.

SEWING ON BUTTONS. Knot the ends of a double thread, and put the needle through the cloth from the upper side to hide the knot under the button. Place a large pin across the button to sew over, draw the thread down loosely until the holes are filled, bring the needle through to the right side under the button, remove the pin, wind the thread several times tightly between the button and the cloth to form a shank, return the needle to the back, and fasten the thread.

To sew on a fancy button of four holes, carry the thread from each of the three holes to one hole, making that the center of three branches.

Some buttons are made with two holes through which a round, woven cord is passed. The ends of the cord are put through an eyelet in the garment and fastened at the back, or a fold of the material is stitched over them. This is done when a long shank is required.

Turn the edges of the 2x4 inch bands, double each lengthwise, baste, and overhand.

(a) Make a ½ inch button-hole at one end of the first band, near the folded edge, and sew a button at the other end.

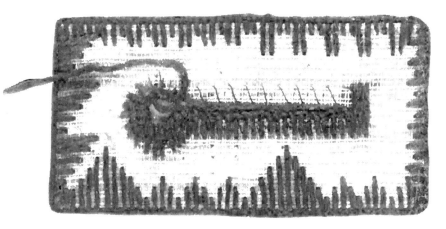

Illustration 23. Button-hole in process of making.

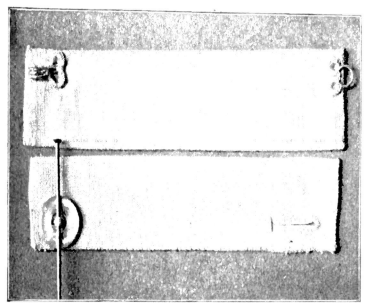

Illustration 24. Represents (a) and (b) of Model 20.

(*b*) Sew a hook on one end of the second band and an eye on the other, in button-hole stitch. (See Illustration 24.)

(*c*) Thread-eyes are bars made of thread and button-holed. They are used to receive hooks or buttons.

Form bars for them by taking stitches to the right and to the left of a ¼ inch space, and cover with button-hole stitches.

(*d*) Eyelets are round holes worked in a garment for ornament or to receive a cord. The holes are made with a bodkin or punch, or cut with scissors.

Make two eyelets, 2 inches apart at the top of the back-stitched design of Model 10, to hold picture cord or ribbon.

Wax a double thread for sewing buttons on garments not to be washed.

Use brass hooks and eyes for wash goods. Test them with a magnet.

If the strain comes on the side of a button-hole, make a bar at both ends. The button-hole of a band should be near the gathers, to be on a line with the strain. The thread should be the size of that in the cloth, and shorter than is used in other sewing.

As button-holes require a great deal of practice, they are taught in separate classes.

Division VI.

MODEL 16. BIAS AND CORNER MATCHING.

Gingham, 5 inches square.

(*a*) Cut a right-angle triangle from the gingham. To do this, begin at middle of one side and cut diagonally through the checks across one corner, fold back the cut edges to match, see that the warp is parallel, and overhand.

49

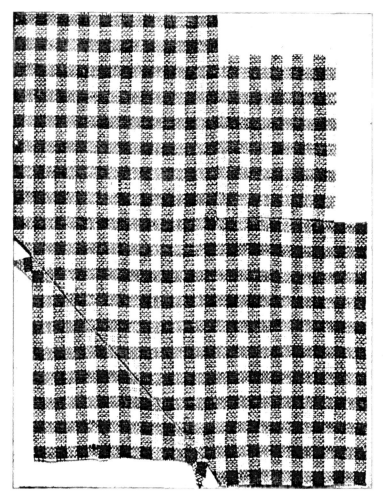

Illustration 25. Gingham matched. Represents Model 16.

Illustration 26. Cloth prepared for Models 17 and 18.

(*b*) Cut a 2 inch square from the opposite corner, fold back the edges to a color line in the gingham, match the square in place as in illustration 25, and overhand.

MODEL 17. OVERHAND PATCH.

Two pieces of checked gingham: 5 inches square; 4 inches square.

Cut from the center of the first a 2 inch square, clip the corners of the opening on the bias, fold back the edges to a color line in the gingham, fold back the edges of the second piece to match, baste one side at a time, and overhand. Trim and overcast the raw edges of the patch and of the opening.

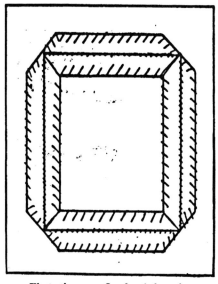

Illustration 27. Overhanded patch.

Illustration 28.
Slash of placket, clipped before sewing.

MODEL 18. HEMMED PATCH.

Follow directions for Model 17 to cut and prepare this model for patching. Baste the 4 inch square on the back to match and hem it to the opening.

Trim the patch to extend ¾ inch beyond this hem, turn in ¼

52

inch, baste, and hem it to the back of the model. When finished, the patch should extend ½ inch beyond the hemmed edge of the opening.

Division VII. Nightshirt Front and Gussets.

MODEL 19. NIGHTSHIRT FRONT AND SHIRTWAIST SLEEVES.

Cotton, 5 inches square.

Two lengthwise pieces of cotton: 1x3 inches for faced hem, and 2½ x3 inches for extension hem.

Double the square parallel with the warp, and cut a 2½ inch slash through the fold. Clip this opening at the angle, as in Illustration 28. Make a faced hem on the right for buttons, and an extension hem on the left for button-holes. The extension hem should be joined so as to fold back on the upper side beyond the seam. Draw a thread near each edge of this fold. Backstitch on these lines and twice across the fold at the angle of the opening.

Make two button-holes, each ⅜ inch in size, on the extension hem, and sew buttons to match on the faced hem.

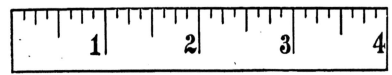

Illustration 29. Inch measure.

MODEL 20. GUSSETS.

Three pieces of cotton: 5 inches square; 1½ inches square; 2 inches square.

(a) Fold the 5 inch square in thirds, parallel to the warp (see Illustration 13). Cut a 2 inch slash at the top of one fold, and the same length at the bottom of the other, and make a narrow hem on each side of both openings.

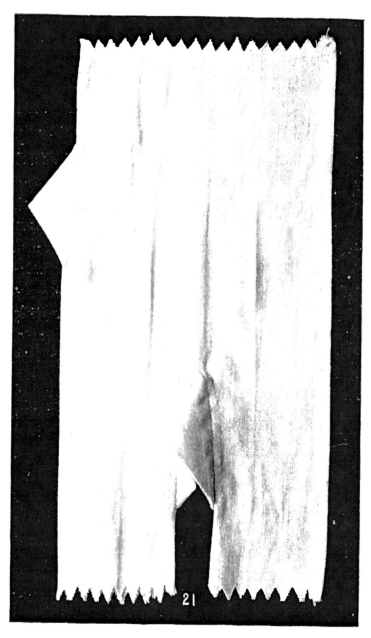

Illustration 30.   Represents Model 20.

Turn all the edges of the 1½ inch square, cut off the corners that are not needed and would make the work thick, double the square into a triangle, baste, insert the right angle of it into one of the openings, and overhand in place.

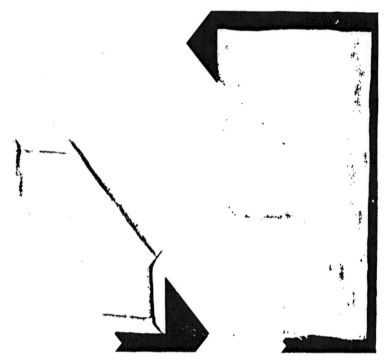

Illustration 31. (*a*) and (*b*).
Gusset cut of paper, and wrong side of a finished gusset.

(*b*) Cut and make the second gusset in paper before making it in cloth. Turn the edges of the 2 inch square, fold the opposite corners over so that their straight sides will measure 1 inch, cut off one of these corners, overhand the other corner into the opening, baste what remains of the square to the back of the model, and hem.

A gusset is used to strengthen the angle of an opening.

55

LIST OF STITCHES.

The ends of a doll's towel are hemstitched and ornamented with rows of different stitches in red marking cotton, if a bedroom outfit is made.

PART THIRD.

Division VIII. Darning.

MODEL 21. WEAVING ON CARDBOARD AND DARNING ON STOCKINET.

Cardboard and stockinet, 2x3 inches.

Practice on small cardboard looms if school looms are not provided.

Doll's Rug. Mount a warp of carpet twine on a loom or weaving frame. A thin needle is made of wood to draw in the woof and press it down. An inch strip of cardboard, woven in first, makes a brace for the woof and retains one inch of the warp for tying.

(*a*) Cover 1 inch square of the center of the cardboard with bars of woolen yarn. Weave the yarn through them to imitate cloth. Wax the end of zephyr to be threaded into a round-eyed needle; fold over the end for a zephyr needle.

(*b*) Darn a piece of stockinet.

MODEL 22. FRENCH HEM, AND DARNING ON TABLE LINEN.

Canvas, 3 inches square.

Table linen, 5 inches square.

(*a*) Button-hole the edge of the canvas with zephyr or silk, and darn a twilled square, 1 inch in size, in the center. The warp threads are taken on the needle, two and two, each two being made up of one under thread and one over thread, so as to form a twill.

Children overcast the canvas for this model.

Teach the square knot with a large, soft cord.

Make holders, and tie them with square knots.

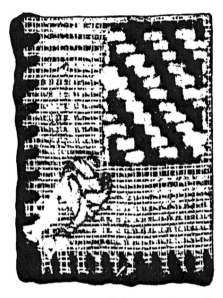 

Illustration 32 (*a*). Twilled weave and square knot.　Illustration 32 (*b*). Square knot.

(*b*) Draw threads for cutting the linen. Fold ¼ inch hems, cut superfluous cloth from corners, turn back, baste, and overhand closely. Use No. 80 thread and No. 9 needle. Fold the model into four sections, measure 1 inch square on one of them, cut it half out and darn in place. Cut ½ inch square from the diagonal section and darn it in plain or twilled weave.

Worn napkins of good quality may be used. Darn with fine linen floss, or with threads drawn from the warp of new linen.

It is sometimes better to wash linen, or wet it in soap-suds, and dry it without rinsing, before hemming it or drawing threads. Rub the sharp edge of a piece of hard soap on threads that are to be drawn.

Darning, cross-stitch and feather-stitch are taught in a special class.

STITCHES ON ILLUSTRATION 33.

1. Right side of Flannel-stitch.
2. Running Outline Stitch.
3. Kensington Stitch.
4, 5, 6, 7. Varieties in Chain-stitch.

8. French Dots.
9, 10. Feather-stitch.
11. Chain-stitch.

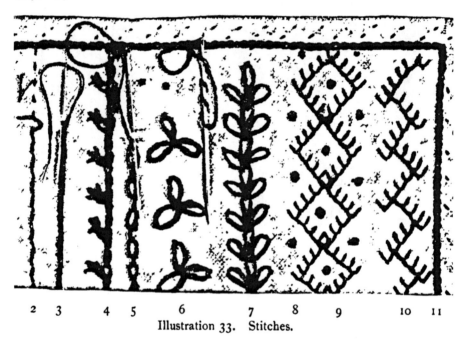

2   3   4   5   6   7   8   9   10   11
Illustration 33.   Stitches.

STITCHES ON ILLUSTRATION 34.   PAGE 60.

1. Chain-stitch.
2 and 3. Feather-stitch.
4. Button-hole Stitch.
5. Herring-bone Stitch.
6. Purl Edge.
7. Blanket-stitch.
8. Flannel-stitch.
9. Cat-stitch.

10. Running and Half-backstitch.
11. Half-backstitch.
12. Backstitch.
13. Hemming.
14. Basting.
15. Overcasting.
16. Running.

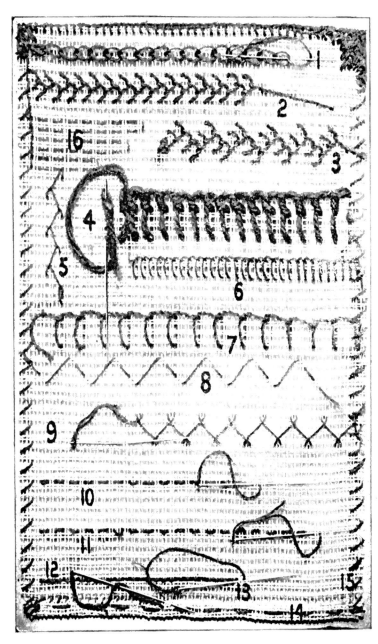

Illustration 34. Stitches named on page 61.

Division IX. Fancy Stitches.

MODEL 23. CHAIN, FEATHER, HERRING-BONE, KENSINGTON, OUTLINE AND FAGOTING STITCHES.

Heavy unbleached cotton or butcher's linen, 5 inches square.

Sheer linen or lawn, 7 inches square.

CHAIN–STITCH. (See Illustration 34. No. 1.) Use red marking cotton. Fasten the thread, hold it down to the left, put the needle in at the end of the last stitch, and sew through the loop.

FEATHER–STITCH. (See Illustration 34. Nos. 2 and 3.)

Hold the thread as in chain-stitch, and follow the designs.

HERRING–BONE STITCH. A feather-stitch, with longer arms and shorter leaves. (See Illustration 34. No. 5.) These stitches can be learned on paper or dotted calico.

KENSINGTON STITCH is a backstitch made backward instead of forward, each stitch passing the last so as to form a double line of stitches. (See Illustration 33.)

RUNNING OUTLINE STITCH is made by passing a thread through each one of a row of running stitches. (See Illustration 33.)

FAGOTING is cat-stitching or making bundles of thread between two edges of cloth. It is also an openwork stitch made on sheer linen or muslin. (See Illustrations 35 and 36.)

(*a*) Draw a single thread from each side of the linen, ½ inch from the edges, and chain-stitch on the lines. Fold the edges back ¼ inch, and hold them in place with flannel-stitch. (See Illustration 34. No. 8.) Fill the center with patterns of feather-stitching.

Any small article which illustrates these stitches will represent this model.

(*b*) Make a doily of the 7 inch square by running a row of stitches one inch from the edge and another in a circle around the centre, 4½ inches in diameter. The hem is attached after the work is done. Use 100 thread and a No. 4 needle. The running stitches

61

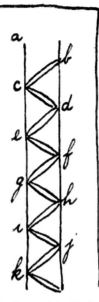

Illustration 35 (*a*). Method of
fagoting on lawn, enlarged.

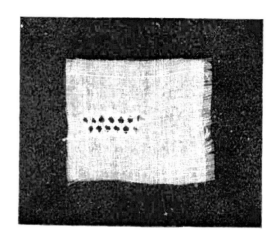

Illustration 35 (*c*). Thread drawn closely after each stitch.

Illustration 35 (*b*). Fagoting with fine thread on
Sheer Lawn.

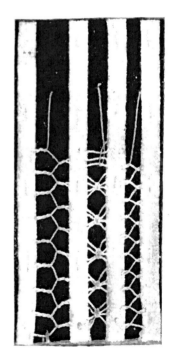

Illustration 36. Fagoting with coarse
thread to join bands.

are a guide and centre line for the work. (See Illustration 35 *a*.) Take up a stitch (*a*) to (*c*), sew through twice, and once from (*b*) to (*c*). Sew through (*b*) to (*d*) twice and once from (*c*) to (*d*). When used on a straight line, two threads may be drawn for guides. Fagoting is used for hems, simple designs and initials.

MODEL 24. SLIP-STITCH OR BLIND HEM, PURL EDGE OR DARNING ON CASHMERE.

Cashmere, 4x5 inches.

SLIP-STITCH OR BLIND HEM. Fold, baste, and take up as little of the cloth with the needle as possible, pass a long stitch inside the fold, and begin the next where the last one ends.

PURL EDGE. Make a line of running stitches, fasten the thread at the left, take the stitches closely together over the line and at right angles to it, and carry the thread from the last stitch under the needle. (See Illustration 34. No. 6.) Baste on oil-cloth while working the edge.

Make a bias and a right angle tear in the cashmere. Draw a thread from the warp of the goods, wax the end to make it thread easily, darn in fine stitches parallel with the woof, then with the warp, weaving the thread at the back of the cloth so as to show as little as possible on the front side.

Finish the sides with purl edge in floss. Slip-stitch a ¼ inch hem at the ends.

A hair is used for very fine darning. Thread the needle with the end drawn from the head.

MODEL 25. BLANKET, FLANNEL AND CAT STITCHES.

Two pieces of flannel: 4x5 inches; 2 inches square.

BLANKET-STITCH is the same as used for purl edge, and is made with spaces between each stitch. Practice the blanket-stitch on the folded edge of cotton cloth, and on the flannel leaves of a needle-book, and a piece of felt or broadcloth for the cover. (See Illustration 34. No. 7.) Flannel and cat stitches are used to secure the raw edges of flannel.

CAT-STITCH is made over the left forefinger upward, instead of downward. Two imaginary parallel lines are followed. The stitches are taken, first on one line, then on the other, each the width of the stitch, higher. (See Illustration 34. No. 9.)

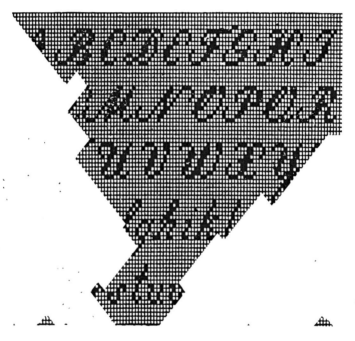

Illustration 37.   Letters in cross-stitch.

FLANNEL-STITCH.   Begin at the edge, and take two running stitches slanting toward the left, carry the thread on a slanting line to the right, and take the stitches as before. (See Illustration 34. No. 8.)

Cut I inch square from the center of the first piece, baste the second on evenly for a patch, join it on the right side with cat-stitch

64

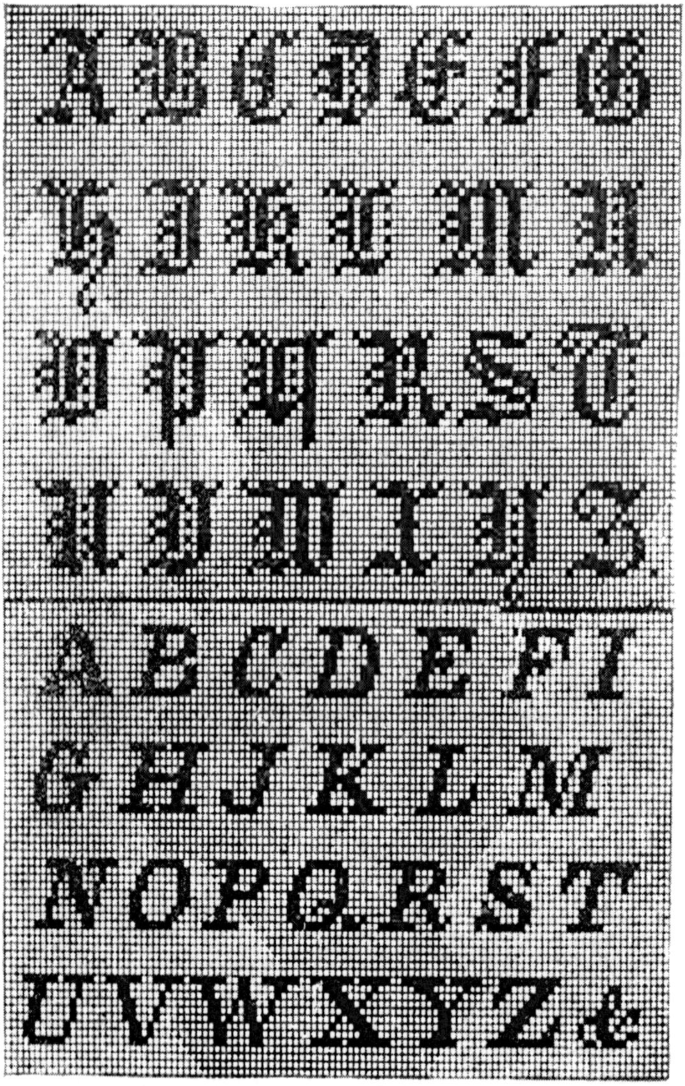

Illustration 38. Letters in cross-stitch.

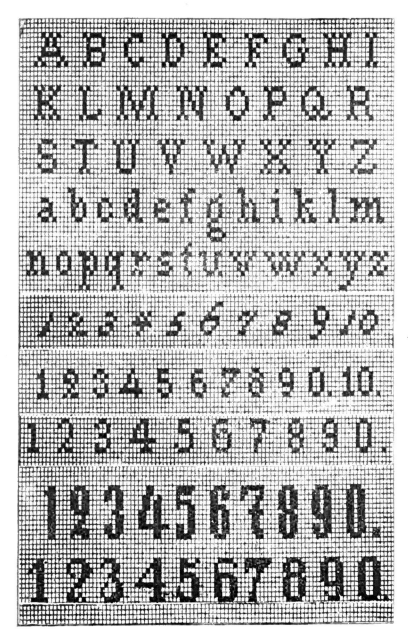

Illustration 39. Letters and figures in cross-stitch.

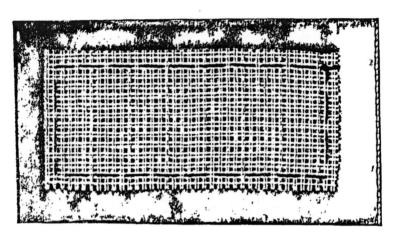

Illustration 40 (*a*). Canvas basted on cloth for cross-stitch.

and on the back with flannel-stitch. Finish the edges of the model with blanket-stitch.

Seams in flannel should be pressed open and the edges fastened back with cat-stitch or flannel-stitch. A tear in firm woolen cloth may be mended by overhanding the torn edges in fine, close stitches on the wrong side. Scratch the nap lightly over the seam with the needle, dampen, and press. '

MODEL 26. PUPIL'S NAME IN CROSS-STITCH.

The first set of stitches cross diagonally in one direction, and the second set in the opposite direction.

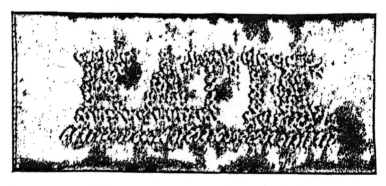

Illustration 40 (*b*). Pupil's name in cross-stitch.

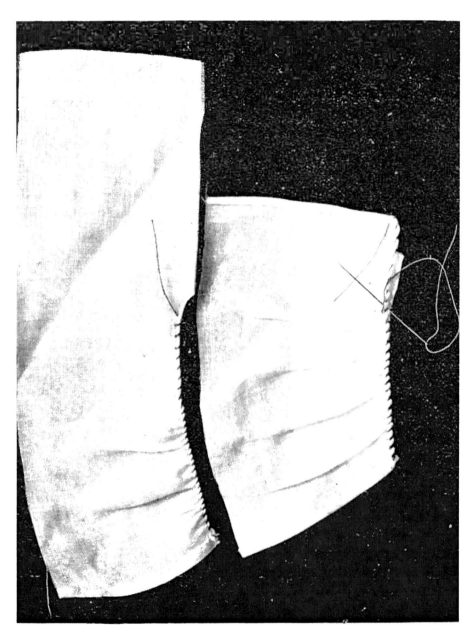

Illus ration 41. (a) and (b). Rolled gathers, and method of sewing them on.

Division X. Rolled Hems, Rolled Gathers, and Sewing on Lace.

MODEL 27. ROLLED HEMS AND ROLLED GATHERS.

Two lengthwise pieces of cotton, 2x4 inches, with selvedge edges. Nainsook, 1x6 inches, for a ruffle. Lace, 7 inches.

Use No. 70 thread for the first two pieces and to gather and join the ruffle. Use No. 100 thread and No. 11 needle for the ruffle.

Overhand the selvedge edges, roll and hem the opposite sides, and finish the ends with ¼ inch hem at the top, and ½ inch hem at the bottom.

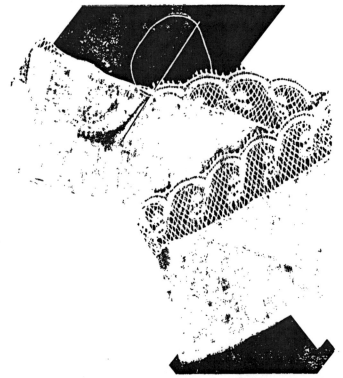

Illustration 42. Sewing lace on a rolled hem.

Overhand the ruffle to the ½ inch hem. Hold the gathers toward you, sew through each, and carry the thread between them for the next stitch.

Practice, by sewing lace on the rolled edge of a handkerchief or a ruffle, before making the model.

Illustration 43. Represents Model 27.

Roll and hem the ends of the ruffle, roll one edge between the left forefinger and thumb, and overhand it to the lace. Roll the opposite edge tightly for gathers, and sew over and over it loosely for the space of an inch, and draw the thread. Roll, and continue as before.

A rolled hem is for fine goods, and is the narrowest that is made. If lace is to be fulled on, take two stitches in the lace to one in the hem, or draw it with a thread.

Division XI

The following models are made for practice during the course:

MODEL 28. DOLL'S GORED SKIRT. (See Page 23.)
MODEL 29. DOLL'S UNDERWAIST. (See page 24.)
MODEL 30. DOLL'S DRAWERS. (See page 24.)
MODEL 31. DOLL'S FLANNEL SKIRT. (See Page 25.)
MODEL 32. DOLL'S DRESS. (See Page 26.)

Division XII.

Pupils who have taken this course are prepared to learn garment making by hand or machine. Pupils in this division have had some practice in cutting and will be able to cut plain garments from patterns. Care should be taken to cut the cloth economically, facings with warps parallel to the parts to be faced, bands lengthwise, and to clip all corners to be turned in.

Small pieces of a garment should be pinned together when cut, also when the work is put away. The first piece is often used as a pattern or measure. By using different pieces, the parts become unequal in size. Careful attention should be paid to joining the parts and to the needles and threads used.

A longer needle is required for running than for other work.

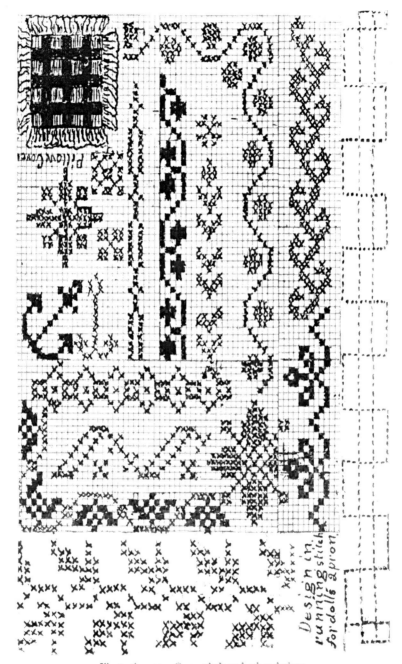

Illustration 44. Cross-stitch and other designs.

DRAFTING CHILDREN'S GARMENTS

The pattern is reduced to one-quarter of the correct size. The measurements are in inches. Take them as follows and write them in a note book under name of child.

Neck, 11.

Bust, measured loosely, 28.

Waist, measured loosely, 26.

Under arm, 7.

Length of back, 13.

Length of front, 13.

Length of shoulder, 6.

Skirt length, 18 in back, 17 in front.

Length of sleeve, under side, 15, upper side, 18 or 20, according to length of shoulder seam.

Wrist band, 8.

No allowance is made on waist pattern for seams or to lap in the back. Two more inches of the bust measure is allowed for the front than for the back, 15 front and 13 back equal 28 bust measure.

The waist line measures 16 in front — one more than at the bust line. 16 front and 10 back equal 26. An inch is added for fullness. If to be gathered into a band and more fullness is required, cut a plain waist pattern, put the point B on the edge of the fold and carry L back to give the fullness required, but do not enlarge the pattern at the under arm seams for that purpose.

Use strong Manila paper for patterns. From these other sizes can be easily cut by applying the measurements.

MEASUREMENTS FOR FRONT OF WAIST.

Measure from the left hand corner 2½ inches along the front edge, dot and mark A–B. Measure 1½ inches along the left edge

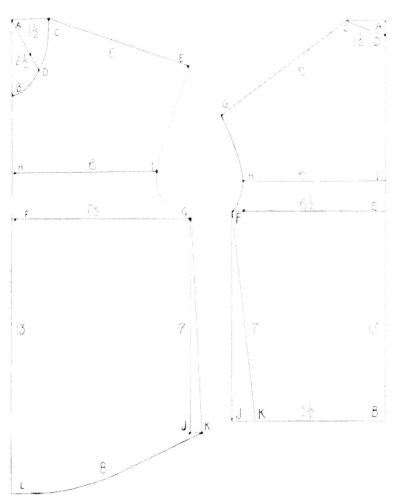

Illustration 45. Pattern of plain waist drafted for eight year old child.

from A, dot and mark C. Measure 2 inches diagonally from A to D for the curve of the neck, and draw the curved line C–D–B. Fold a circle of paper into twenty-four sections, and use one as a guide to slope the shoulder. Lay it along the left edge with the point at C and draw the 6 inch line C–E. (This slope is also obtained by drawing fifteen degrees of a circle. Begin 2 inches from the neck, to curve this line upward so as to add ¼ inch on each side of the front to the neck size.

Measure from B to the point crossed by the bust line and mark it F. (B–F measures 4 inches.) Measure from F at right angles to the front, a 7½ inch line to G. Begin at the front 1½ inches above this and draw a 6 inch line, H–I. Curve the line from E to I slightly and make a deep curve from I to G.

Draw a 7 inch line from G to J parallel to the front. Measure ½ inch to the right from J to K and draw a slanting line from G to K for the under arm seam.

MEASUREMENTS FOR BACK OF WAIST

Draw a 13 inch line for opening at the back, and mark it A–B. Measure 1¾ inches at right angles to A–B from A to C. Draw a curved line from C to D, taking off ½ inch of A–B. Fold a circle of paper into twelve sections and use one for the slope of the shoulder. Lay it along the left edge with the point at C and draw the 6 inch line, C–G. Measure 6 inches from B to E and draw a 6½ inch line from E to F, at right angles to A–B. Draw a 6 inch line one inch above E–F, beginning on the line A–B, and mark it H–I. Draw a curved line through G–H–F for the back of the armsize. Draw the 7 inch line F–J, parallel to E–B, also the line J–B. Measure 1 inch from J toward B and mark K. Draw the line F–K for the under arm seam. This pattern will lap slightly at the back on a straight figure.

Apply arm measurements to a pattern of the required style, to get the different sizes. For a close fitting sleeve, take measurements around the arm, above and below the elbow and near the shoulder; also the length each way from the elbow. Cut the under side $\frac{2}{8}$ the width of the upper, curve the top of the under arm piece slightly and round the upper side according to the length of the shoulder, cutting both so that the back seam is $2\frac{1}{2}$ inches longer than the front seam (of the sleeve) at the top and a half inch longer at the bottom. The front seam curves from top to wrist, one inch toward the sleeve; the back seam slopes from the elbow to the wrist enough to give the right size for the hand.

The front arm seam is joined to the front of the arm-size half way between I and G. The sleeve should be carefully hung and the arm-size enlarged (if necessary) below the mark I, and as little under the arm as possible.

Fold cloth at *d* for sleeve; at *c* for front of skirt. Join *a* and *b*. Allow on skirt and sleeve for length and fullness. Add two inches to width of skirt for reversed box pleat under the arm, to be left loose below the arm size or stitched together one inch.

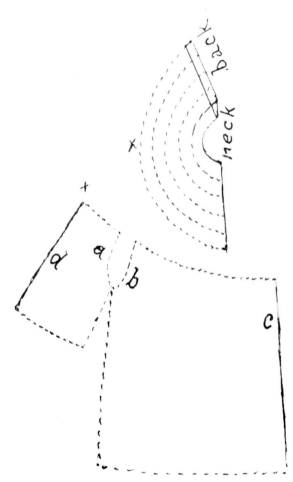

Illustration 46. Pattern for doll's dress.

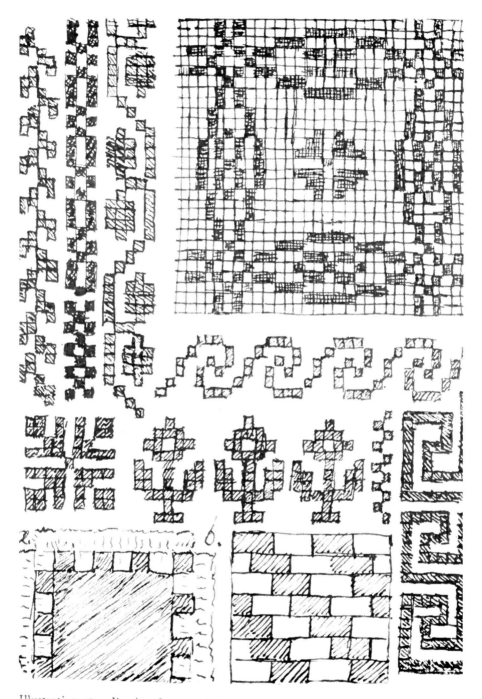

Illustration 47.   Bead and cross-stitch patterns.   (*a*) and (*b*) Sofa pillow covers.

FINGER EXERCISES

The correct position of the hands, implements, and work for sewing are of great importance.

The exercise of threading a needle and tying a knot should be given when the class opens. When it is well learned, others may be taught, as pupil's advance.

FIRST EXERCISE — THREADING A NEEDLE AND TYING A KNOT.

Use a medium size thread with a coarse needle that will thread easily.

(a) Sit upright and hold the thread up in the left hand.

(b) Roll the end of the thread between the right thumb and forefinger to twist it.

(c) Hold up the eye of the needle between the tips of the right thumb and forefinger, with thread in the left hand in the same manner.

(d) Put the thread into the eye of the needle, and draw through ⅓ of its length with the left thumb and forefinger.

(e) Catch both threads and swing the needle under the middle joint of the thimble finger.

(f) Slide the left thumb and forefinger to the long end of the thread and pass it to the right thumb and forefinger.

(g) Wind it once around the finger, roll it slightly with the thumb, and draw it up with the third finger.

Repeat this exercise until a knot can be well made.

Second Exercise — The Position of the Needle and Thimble for the Overhand Stitch.

Place the folded edge of a piece of cloth between the left thumb and forefinger, and a thimble on the thimble finger. Use a threaded needle without a knot.

(*a*) Hold the needle at the tips of the right thumb and forefinger.

(*b*) Put the needle against the thimble.

(*c*) Insert the needle in the folded edge of the cloth (see Model 2 (*a*), and point directly toward you.

(*d*) Use the side of the thimble and push the needle through the cloth. Repeat this exercise.

Illustration 48. The thimble finger holding the needle, while the thumb and forefinger are tying the knot, or preparing work.

Third Exercise — Making the Running Stitch.

The thread should have no knot. Take two or three running stitches in a piece of cloth.

(*a*) Hold the piece up in the right hand, with the forefinger on one side of the edge and the thumb on the other, holding the needle and edge closely between them.

(*b*) Push the needle with the thimble and take up stitches at the same time, using the left thumb and forefinger as a guide for the stitches and to hold the cloth, and not to fill the needle.

(c) Draw the thread through. Repeat this exercise at each lesson until it is well learned.

Drills on the other stitches may be given in the same manner, as pupils advance. In giving drills, the teacher stands with her left side to the class and holds her hands to the right, so that all can see the movements.

Crosswise Basting.

Illustration 49. Basting — One-quarter inch stitches, with one-inch spaces.

CLOTH REQUIRED FOR TWENTY SETS OF MODELS.

Dotted calico, Model 1 . . . . $\frac{3}{4}$ yd.

Dotted calico for feather-stitch practice . . . . . . 1 yd.

   The spaces between dots are measured lengthwise.

Figured calico, Models 2 and 4 in two colors, of each . . $\frac{1}{2}$ yd.

Calico with figures having direction, Model 6 . . . $1\frac{1}{8}$ yds.

Striped calico or gingham, Models 3, 5, and 7 . . . . $1\frac{1}{8}$ yds.

Quarter inch check gingham, Models 6, 16, 17, and 18 . . $2\frac{3}{4}$ yds.

Heavy unbleached cotton for design in backstitch, Model 10 . $\frac{1}{2}$ yd.

Medium grade of same for design in running, Model 5 . . . $\frac{1}{3}$ yd.

Half bleached cotton models . . . . 6 yds.

Long cloth, Model 27 and doll's clothes . . . . $2\frac{1}{2}$ yds.

Canvas Models 22, 26 . . . . $\frac{1}{2}$ yd.

Table Linen, Model 22 . . . . $3\frac{1}{2}$ sq. ft.

Butcher's Linen, Model 23 . . . . $\frac{1}{2}$ yd.

Flannel, Model 24 . . . . 3.2 sq. ft.

Cashmere, Model 25 . . . . 2.8 sq. ft.

These estimates are made for twenty-five inch calico and gingham, and for yard wide cotton.

Two yards of bright calico, in contrasting colors, will supply a class of twenty with patchwork for dolls' bedspreads. Fourteen yards each of turkey red and bright blue calico will make twenty sofa-pillow covers, fifteen inches square, with ruffles and backs.

OUTLINE FOR A TWO YEARS' COURSE.

MODELS 1, 2 (b), 3, 5; DOLL'S APRON — 6 (a), 7 (a), 8 (a) and (b), 9, 10; AND BACKSTITCH DESIGN — 11, 12 (a), 13 (a) and (b), 14 (a) and (b), 15 (a) (b) (c) and (d), 16, 17, 18, 21 (a) and (b).

Practice is given on small garments and articles for use. Feather-stitch and cross-stitch are taught on them. A set of doll's garments are made.

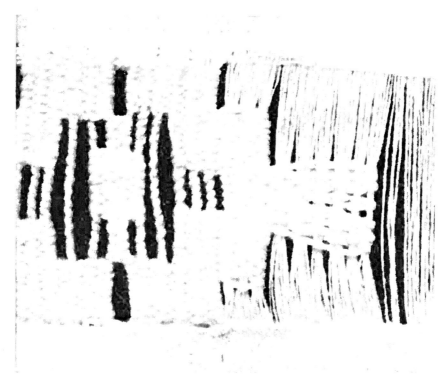

Illustration 50 (a). Fayal weaving enlarged.

Use Cotton Perle, No. 8 (Dollfus, Mieg & Co.), for weaving. Sew over and over the clusters of threads to form the cords and pass the needle inside the weaving to reach the next cluster when one is covered. Baste on oilcloth. Use a hoop and blunt needle.

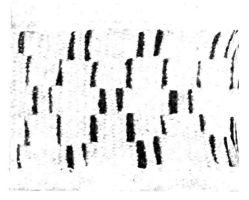

Illustration 50 (b). Fayal weaving.

PIECES REQUIRED FOR ONE SET OF MODELS.

Model 1. Quarter inch dotted calico, 4 x 7 in.

Model 2. Two colors of calico, each 2 x 4 in. Two pieces of cotton each, 2 x 4 in.

Model 3. Two pieces of striped calico or gingham, each 2 x 4 inches.

Model 4. Four pieces of calico in two colors, two pieces of each, $2\frac{1}{2}$ in. sq.

Model 5. Striped calico or gingham 5 in. sq. Medium unbleached cotton, $2\frac{1}{2}$ x 6 in.

Model 6. Checked gingham, 5 in. sq. Calico with upright designs, 5 x 8 in.

Model 7. Striped calico or gingham, 2 x 4 in. Half-bleached cotton, 6 x 8 in.

Model 8. Two pieces half-bleached cotton, each 5 in. sq.

Model 9. Half-bleached cotton with selvedge, 6 x $6\frac{1}{2}$ in.

Model 10. Two pieces half-bleached cotton, 5 in. sq., $2\frac{1}{2}$ x 5 in. Firm unbleached cotton, 5 in. sq.

Model 11. Half-bleached cotton, 5 in. sq.

Model 12. Same, 5 in. sq., $1\frac{1}{2}$ in. sq., $2\frac{1}{2}$ x $1\frac{1}{2}$ in.

Model 13. Same, 5 in. sq., 1 x $4\frac{1}{2}$ in.

Model 14. Same, 5 in. sq., $2\frac{1}{4}$ x 1 in., $2\frac{1}{4}$ x $1\frac{1}{2}$ in.

Model 15. Firm bleached cotton, 2 x 6 in. Two pieces of same, each 2 x 4 in.

Model 16. Checked gingham, 5 in. sq.

Model 17. Two pieces same, 5 in. sq., 4 in. sq.

Model 18. Two pieces same, 5 in. sq., 4 in. sq.

Model 19. Half-bleached cotton, 5 in sq., 1 x 3 in., $2\frac{1}{2}$ x 3 in.

Model 20. Half-bleached cotton, 5 in. sq., 2 in. sq., $1\frac{1}{2}$ in. sq.

Model 21. Cardboard and stockinet, 2 x 3 in.

Model 22. Canvas, 3 in. sq., quarter inch cord, 1 ft.

Model 23. Butcher's linen, 5 in. sq.

Model 24. Cashmere, 4 x 5 in.

Model 25. Two pieces of flannel, 4 x 5 in., 2 in. sq.

Model 26. Canvas 2 x 5 in., ribbon $\frac{1}{4}$ yd.

Model 27. Two pieces of long cloth, with selvedge, 2 x 4 in. Nainsook, 1 x 6 in., lace, 7 inches.

Model 28. Muslin.

Model 29. Long cloth

Model 30. Long cloth.

Model 31. Outing flannel.

Model 32. White India linon or lawn.

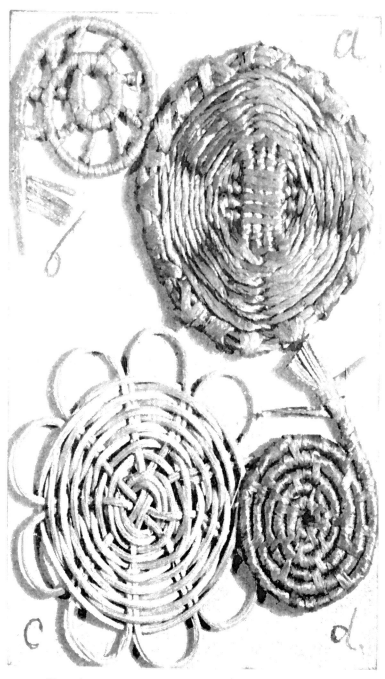

Illustration 51. (a) and (b) Reed and raffia. (c) Reed (d) Raffia.

AMERICAN INDIAN BEAD WORK AND BASKETRY.

BEAD WORK.

FRAMES.. The simplest frames for bead work are made of two blocks of wood, one inch in width and thickness and three inches long, one square inch by three inches, and two half inch boards two inches wide and two feet long. A double row of brads are nailed into one side of each block, one quarter of an inch apart and so placed that the brads of one row are opposite the spaces of the other. Make the boards adjustable by joining them with movable bolts and nail the blocks across the ends with the brads extending upward or outward. If greater length is required, extend the warp between and beyond the brads and wind it about the ends of the frame.

For wider work, make an oblong frame with brads at each end. This frame is used by children for weaving raffia and rags. Frames for children's use are cut from heavy cardboard, with small holes made at the ends to carry the warp. Looms for school and home use are kept in kindergarten and school supply stores.

MATERIAL. No. 60 Barbour's linen thread, 300 ball thread, 36 cotton, or a corresponding size of twist, are used for the warp, and 60 cotton for the woof. The objection to using silk for the woof is that the knots work loose. Thread wears better if it is waxed. As wax holds the dust it should not be used for white beads. Join threads with a square or a weavers' knot. Use a No. 12 needle and a single thread for fine beads. Reject those that are not of the regular size, such as thick, thin, and uneven ones. Indians prefer the opaque beads.

WEAVING. Put one more thread on the warp than the number of spaces required and draw until it is tight. Thread the end coming from the spool and tie the other end to the thread of the warp that is nearest the weaver, string the number of beads for a row, pass the needle under the warp and the beads under and at right angles to it, press one bead into each space with the left forefinger and return the needle through the beads above the warp, so that the thread passes through them twice, once below and once above. Do not draw the thread of the woof tight but press the woven beads against the row above. This makes the texture smooth, soft, and firm, and does not give too much strain on the woof.

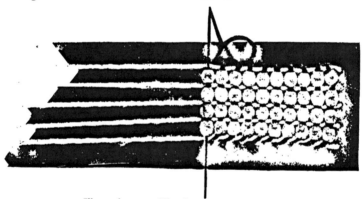

Illustration 52. Weaving beads, enlarged.

Two needles are used for wide bead work, one to carry the beads below the warp and one to pass through them above it. By this means the work can be handled better and mistakes in a line of beads can be easily corrected. The needle that is used to pass through the beads above the warp is used to string the beads for the next row.

FINISHING. Fasten the thread by running it back through a row or more of beads. Tie the warp with a square knot in sets of

90

two closely to the last row of beads. Thread one of each set and carry it through or between several of the beads of the texture and cut it off. String each of the remaining threads with the coarser beads to the required length for a fringe, pass the needle back through all but the last bead and fasten the end thread to the texture by two or three button-hole stitches.

Illustration 53. Three ply Raffia Braid.

BASKETRY.

MATERIALS. Reeds are the stems of coarse grasses that grow in wet places and are common in America and Europe.

Raffia is a palm of Madagascar, with very large leaves having a fibrous cuticle. The prepared fiber is also called raffia. It is used for mats, tie bands, baskets, and fancy articles. The natural color is cream white. Reed, wire, cord, and twisted raffia are used as foundations for Indian baskets. Raffia is a substitute for the fine material, not easily obtained, which is dyed by Indians and used with cheaper fiber back of it to give body to the texture. Dyed porcupine quills and the colored feathers of birds are also used for patterns. The color is carried along the cord or reed when not required.

A book on Indian Basketry has been issued by the Smithsonian Institute, Washington, D. C., and is sent free of charge to those who are making a study of this art.

Illustration 54.   Three ply Braid woven with Reeds.

BASKET MAKING. Reed baskets are easily made. The reeds are soaked in warm water for fifteen minutes, if they are fine. Eight are cut the desired length. Several inches are allowed to turn in for the border.

A REED MAT is the first piece made. The reeds are crossed in the center, four at right angles to four. Some basket makers cut slits along the center of four through which the other four are passed. The end of a reed, called the weaver, is inserted and is carried around the center, starting under the lower four and passing over the upper four from left to right twice around to hold them firmly in place. Another spoke is added to make an uneven number. The weaver is pressed closely each time that it is carried around between the spokes until the mat is of the required size. The ends are then trimmed and turned in to form a border.

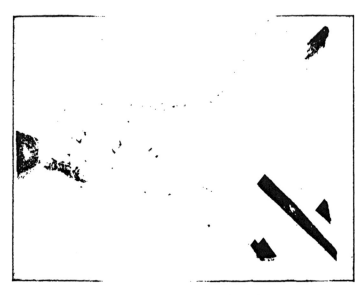

Illustration 55. Nine ply Raffia Braid.

A reed basket is started in the same manner. Bend up the spokes when the bottom is between three and four inches in diameter and weave around them to form the sides of the basket. After some skill is acquired, two or more weavers can be used at a time. For

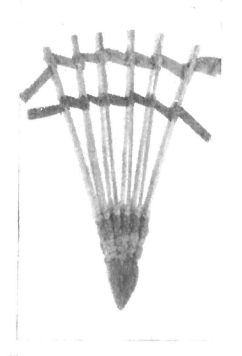

Illustration 56. Raffia and Reed or Wire, No. 1.

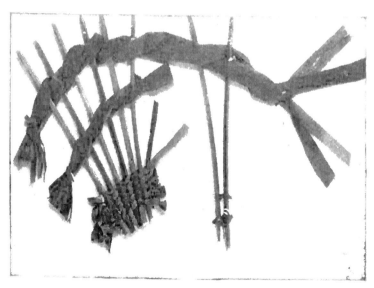

Illustration 57. Raffia and Reed or Wire, No. 2.

larger baskets, more spokes are added. When within several inches of the top, trim the reeds evenly and carry them forward and down beside the third or fourth reed to form the border, if they are thick, or beside the second reed if only the nine spokes are used.

RAFFIA BASKETS. Dyed raffia is rolled in a damp cloth to moisten it, the uncolored may be soaked. As it is thin at the ends

Illustration 58. A twisted cord of raffia wound and sewed with raffia.

it is lapped when joined. The strips should be kept uniform in size for weaving. Lap at intervals when making a braid of raffia.

Wind from left to right and sew through from back to front. Form a small ring of the end of the cord. Thread a strip of raffia into a darning needle and sew around the ring until it is covered. Pass the raffia around the cord twice, and through or around the preceding row from the back to the front, and draw it up until the cords meet. Continue to pass the raffia twice around the cord, and once around it and the preceding row or through the latter.

To separate the rows of cord with rows of openwork, draw up the strip of raffia so that the cords will be one quarter of an inch apart and sew around this thread from right to left to form a shank.

Baskets are made in the same manner by using reed ⅛ inch in diameter, and making longer spaces and shorter shanks.

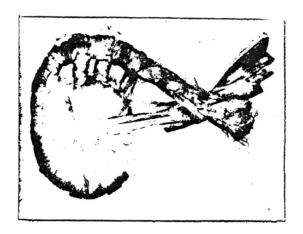

Illustration 59.   Raffia and cord with rows of openwork.

The illustrations show several modes of making baskets.   When two strands are used at a time they are crossed at the back.

In illustration 57, the five lower rows, in two colors, are woven the same as the upper two.   White raffia is carried at the back of each colored strip to give body to it.

INDEX

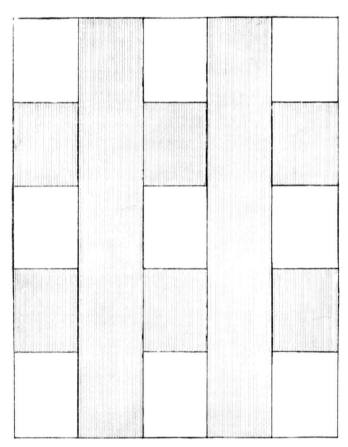

Illustration 60.   Design for patch-work pillow of strips and $3\frac{1}{2}$ inch squares for young pupils.

Illustration 61.   Design for stitching;   also to be enlarged for sofa pillow cover.

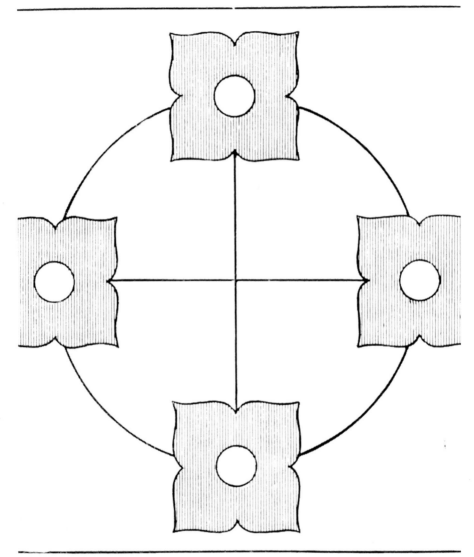

Illustration 62.   Design for stitching; also to be enlarged for sofa pillow cover.

ImTheStory.com

CPSIA information can be obtained at www.ICGtesting.com
Printed in the USA
LVOW120002030713

341301LV00005B/136/P